Sports Illustrated KIDS

A SUPERFAN'S GUIDE TO

PRO Basketball TEAMS

▶▶▶▶▶▶▶▶▶▶▶

By Tyler Omoth

CAPSTONE PRESS
a capstone imprint

Sports Illustrated Kids Pro Sports Team Guides are published by Capstone Press, a Capstone Imprint, 1710 Roe Crest Drive, North Mankato, Minnesota 56003. www.capstonepub.com

Library of Congress Cataloging-in-Publication Data
is available on the Library of Congress website:
ISBN: 978-1-5157-8850-8 (library binding)
ISBN: 978-1-5157-8856-0 (eBook PDF)

Editorial Credits
Elizabeth Johnson and Nate LeBoutillier, editors; Terri Poburka, designer; Eric Gohl, media research; Gene Bentdahl, production specialist

Photo Credits
Newscom: Cal Sport Media/Chris Szagola, 23l, 28r, 63l, Cal Sport Media/John Fisher, 39l, Cal Sport Media/Stephen Lew, 53l, EFE/Craig Lassig, 40r, EFE/Kamil Krzaczynski, 9l, 45l, EFE/Monica M. Davey, 32r, EPA/Erik S. Lesser, 22r, EPA/Larry W. Smith, 46r, EPA/Peter Foley, 11l, EPA/Steve Dipaola, 54r, EPA/Tannen Maury, 38r, Icon Sportswire/J.P. Wilson, 21l, Icon Sportswire/Torrey Purvey, 18r, 62r, Splash News/ Charlie Ans, 15l, TNS/Curtis Compton, 7l, 33l, TNS/David Santiago, 36r, TNS/Hector Amezcua, 56r, 57l, TNS/Stephen M. Dowell, 48r, TNS/Steven M. Falk, 50r, 51l, UPI/ Jon Soohoo, 42r, ZUMA Press/Ed Crisostomo, 30r, ZUMA Press/Hector Acevedo, 20r; Shutterstock: Africa Studio, cover (top), Big Pants Production, throughout (basketball), Billion Photos, throughout (shoes), Brocreative, 4–5, Chones, throughout (trophies), CP DC Press, 49l, Mega Pixel, throughout (pennant), Piotr Krzeslak, 66–67bkg, 68–69bkg, 72; Sports Illustrated: Al Tielemans, 3l, 12r, 28l, 61l, Andy Hayt, 9r, 20l, 30l, 32l, 58l, 67r, Bill Frakes, 35r, 64r, Bob Rosato, 3m, 12l, 18l, 36l, 42l, 58r, 60l, 64l, 68ml, Damian Strohmeyer, 8r, 21l, David E. Klutho, 6r, 14r, 17r, 29l, 34l, 37l, 43r, 44r, Heinz Kluetmeier, 39r, 50l, Hy Peskin, 5, 8l, John Biever, 63r, John D. Hanlon, 7r, 10l, 44l, 45r, 68l, John G. Zimmerman, 25r, 68r, John Iacono, 33r, John W. McDonough, cover (bottom), 2l, 2r, 3r, 13l, 16r, 19l, 19r, 24r, 26r, 27l, 27r, 31l, 31r, 34r, 35l, 37r, 41l, 43l, 47l, 47r, 49r, 52l, 52r, 53r, 55l, 59l, 59r, 60r, 62l, 67m, Lane Stewart, 22l, 67l, Manny Millan, 11r, 13r, 14l, 15r, 16l, 23r, 26l, 29r, 46l, 48l, 51r, 55r, 56l, 66l, 66r, Richard Meek, 6l, Robert Beck, 40l, 57r, 66m, Simon Bruty, 2m, 10r, 17l, 25l, 41r, 61r, 65l, Walter Iooss Jr., 24l, 38l, 54l, 65r

Design Elements: Shutterstock

All statistics updated through 2016-17 NBA regular season.

Printed in the United States of America
10953R

TABLE OF CONTENTS

NEVER GET ENOUGH

Ask a Warriors fan who played center for the 1961–62 team, and he'll tell you it was Wilt Chamberlain. Ask a Bulls fan which guard made the series-clinching shot of the 1997 NBA Finals, and she'll tell you it was not Michael Jordan but Steve Kerr. Ask a Thunder fan how many triple doubles Russell Westbrook had in 2016-17, and he'll tell you 42, an NBA record.

Basketball fans are devoted to their favorite teams. They know their team's history and all the players' names and jersey numbers. They're loyal through bad times, always feeling sure things will be different next year. That's what it means to be a fan.

It's something else to be a superfan. What the difference? Superfans want to know it all. They steep themselves in the stories and numbers that tell the story of National Basketball Association (NBA). They track the results of every game from the preseason in October through the playoffs in June. They follow every team. They can't get enough.

Atlanta
HAWKS

The Hawks first took the court for the 1946–47 season as the Tri-Cities Blackhawks in the National Basketball League (NBL). The team joined the NBA in 1949. The team moved to Milwaukee and were renamed the Milwaukee Hawks in 1951. Four years later it was time to move again, this time to St. Louis, where the Hawks played 13 seasons. The Hawks moved to Atlanta in 1968 and have played there ever since.

WON/LOSS RECORD:
2,693–2,695 (.500 W–L%)

HOME COURT:
Philips Arena

SUPERFACT

The Hawks have retired five jersey numbers to honor former greats: number 9 for Bob Pettit, number 21 for Dominique Wilkins, number 23 for Lou Hudson, number 40 for Jason Collier, and number 55 for Dikembe Mutombo. They also honored longtime owner Ted Turner.

Then & Now
BOB PETTIT 1954–65 / PAUL MILLSAP 2013–present

TROPHY CASE

Championships:
1958

Franchise Leaders

Games:
Dominique Wilkins, 882

Points:
Dominique Wilkins, 23,292

Rebounds:
Bob Pettit, 12,849

Steals:
Mookie Blaylock, 1,321

*Free throws made
without a miss, single game:*
Pete Maravich, 18 (1973) •----

SUPERFACT

Growing up in Germany, point guard **Dennis Schroder** didn't spend his free time playing basketball. His passion was riding the rails and ramps on a skateboard at the local skate park. He might have been good enough to go pro, but a basketball coach found him and pushed him to focus his natural athleticism on the court instead. Dennis still skates for fun.

Boston
CELTICS

The Boston Celtics got their start as one of the original teams in the Basketball Association of America (BAA) in 1946. After the BAA and the National Basketball League (NBL) merged, Boston began play in the NBA for the 1949–1950 season. The Celtics have won 17 NBA titles, more than any other franchise. Of their 17 trophies, 11 were won during a remarkable 13-year span from 1957–1969.

WON/LOSS RECORD:
3,274–2,286 (.589 W–L%)

HOME COURT:
TD Garden

SUPERFACT

Hall of Fame center Robert Parish famously wore jersey number 00 throughout his career. He started wearing the number when he was in junior high school. When the basketball team handed out jerseys, he was the last to get one and 00 was the only number left.

Then & Now
BOB COUSEY 1950–63 / AVERY BRADLEY 2010–present

TROPHY CASE

Championships:
1957, 1959, 1960, 1961, 1962, 1963, 1964, 1965, 1966, 1968, 1969, 1974, 1976, 1981, 1984, 1986, 2008

Franchise Leaders:

Games:
John Havlicek, 1,270

Points:
John Havlicek, 26,395

Assists:
Bob Cousey, 6,945

Rebounds:
Bill Russell, 21,620

Points per game, career:
Larry Bird, 24.3

SUPERFACT

Isaiah Thomas got his name because of a bet. His father bet his friend that the Detroit Pistons would lose to the Los Angeles Lakers in the 1989 NBA Finals. At the time, the Pistons point guard was Hall of Fame player Isiah Thomas. Though the Celtics star was born before the Finals took place, the name stuck. The Pistons did go on to win the championship.

Brooklyn NETS

The Brooklyn Nets took the court for the first time in 1967 as a part of the American Basketball Association. The team had several names as it bounced between New York and New Jersey over the decades. The Nets became a part of the NBA in 1976. The team won two ABA championships, but has not yet taken home the trophy as a member of the NBA.

WON/LOSS RECORD:
1,754–2,304 (.432 W–L%)

HOME COURT:
Barclays Center

SUPERFACT

The Nets logo was designed by part-owner of the team and Brooklyn hip-hop music star Jay-Z when the team moved from New Jersey to Brooklyn, New York in 2012. The Nets' previous logos all had shades of red and blue. The newest logo is the first to feature only black and white.

Then & Now
JULIUS ERVING 1973–76 / BROOK LOPEZ 2008–present

TROPHY CASE

Championships:
1974, 1976 (ABA)

Franchise Leaders:

Games:
Buck Williams, 635

Points:
Brook Lopez, 10,444

Rebounds:
Buck Williams, 7,576

Assists:
Jason Kidd, 4,620

Blocks:
Brook Lopez, 972

SUPERFACT

Point guard **Jeremy Lin** likes to bring "Linsanity" to the court, but he has fun before the tip-off, too. Throughout his career, he's developed a number of goofy handshake rituals with different teammates. The handshakes include pretending to put on glasses or flip through books. Some handshakes also include funky dance moves.

Charlotte
HORNETS

The Charlotte Hornets arrived in the NBA as an expansion team for the 1988–89 season. The team moved to New Orleans after the 2001–02 season, but the NBA immediately granted Charlotte another team. In 2004–05, the Charlotte Bobcats tipped off. The new name lasted a decade, but in 2014–15, Charlotte reclaimed the name "Charlotte Hornets." While the franchise has been to the playoffs ten times, they've never made it to the Finals.

WON/LOSS RECORD:
952–1,214 (.440 W–L%)

HOME COURT:
Spectrum Center

SUPERFACT

When the Hornets took the court for the first time, they added another first to the list. Their jerseys were the first in NBA history to feature pinstripes. The colorful uniforms used a combination of white, purple, teal, green, and blue. Several other NBA teams have since created pinstriped versions of their own uniforms.

Then & Now

ADAM MORRISON 2006–09 / MARVIN WILLIAMS 2014–present

TROPHY CASE

Championships:
None

Franchise Leaders:

Games:
Dell Curry, 701

Points:
Dell Curry, 9,839

Rebounds:
Emeka Okafor, 3,516

Assists:
Muggsy Bogues, 5,557

Blocks:
Alonzo Mourning, 684

SUPERFACT

Point guard **Kemba Walker**'s moves on the court open him up for big shots. Off the court, his moves might be even better. Walker started hip-hop and jazz dance lessons at the age of eight. His dance troupe performed in more than one talent show at the famous Apollo Theater in Harlem.

13

Chicago BULLS

The Chicago Bulls tipped off in the 1966–67 season as an expansion franchise in the NBA. Since then, it has been one of the most successful teams in the league. The Bulls have made the playoffs 35 times in 51 seasons. They've even won six championships in two separate "three-peat" title runs.

WON/LOSS RECORD:
2,156–1,977 (.522 W–L%)

HOME COURT:
United Center

SUPERFACT

NBA legend, Michael Jordan's number 23 Chicago Bulls jersey is one of the most popular in NBA history. Jordan's jersey was so popular, that on February 14th, 1990, someone stole his game jersey. Without his regular uniform, the superstar had to play a game wearing a number 12 jersey with no name on the back.

Then & Now

MICHAEL JORDAN 1984–93; 1994–98 / JIMMY BUTLER 2011–prese

TROPHY CASE

Championships:
1991, 1992, 1993, 1996, 1997, 1998

Franchise Leaders:

Games:
Michael Jordan, 930

Points:
Michael Jordan, 29,277

Rebounds:
Michael Jordan, 5,836

Assists:
Michael Jordan, 5,012

Coaching victories:
Phil Jackson, 545

1994 All-Star Game MVP:
Scottie Pippen

SUPERFACT

After playing his first 13 seasons with the Miami Heat, **Dwyane Wade** joined the Bulls in 2016. Wade was born and raised in Chicago and played football and basketball while growing up in the city. Early on, Wade was a better wide receiver than hoopster. The summer before his junior year, Wade sprouted up four inches. The extra height helped. He set basketball records at his high school for points and steals during his senior year.

Cleveland CAVALIERS

The Cleveland Cavaliers joined the NBA in 1970 as an expansion franchise. The Cavs have shown periods of greatness, as well as their share of low points during the franchise's existence. Led by LeBron James and Kyrie Irving, the Cavaliers played in back-to-back NBA finals in 2015 and 2016, winning their first championship in 2016.

WON/LOSS RECORD:
1,779–2,027 (.467 W–L%)

HOME COURT:
Quicken Loans Arena

SUPERFACT

Superstar forward LeBron James has worn the number 23 since childhood in homage to his basketball hero, Michael Jordan. He wore it professionally with the Cavaliers from 2003 to 2010. When he left Cleveland to play for the Miami Heat, he adopted a new jersey number, 6. Upon his return to Cleveland, James donned number 23 once again saying that he'd earned the right to wear his hero's number after winning two NBA Championships with the Heat.

Then & Now
BRAD DAUGHERTY 1986–94 / TRISTAN THOMPSON 2011–present

TROPHY CASE

Championships:
2016

Franchise Leaders:
Games:
Zydrunas Ilgauskas, 771

Points:
LeBron James, 20,868

Rebounds:
Zydrunas Ilgauskas, 5,904

Assists:
LeBron James, 5,481

Points in a single game:
Kyrie Irving, 57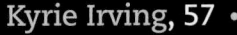

SUPERFACT

LeBron James is all business on the court. But when he has free time, he likes to watch cartoons. Tom & Jerry and Spongebob Squarepants are two of his favorites. The superstar has even been known to switch the locker room TV from NBA highlights to Teen Titans Go!

Dallas
MAVERICKS

The Dallas Mavericks joined the NBA in 1980. The successful franchise has made the playoffs in 21 of 37 seasons and taken home one NBA Championship trophy. Over the three and a half decades, the Mavs have been home to some of the league's greatest stars like Derek Harper, Steve Nash, Rolando Blackman, and Dirk Nowitzki.

WON/LOSS RECORD:
1,515–1,471 (.507 W–L%)

HOME COURT:
American Airlines Center

SUPERFACT

Before the 2015–16 season, Dallas Mavericks owner Mark Cuban held a contest for fans. He challenged fans to design a team uniform for the Mavs. The winning submission by Geoff Case was made into a reality and donned by the team in several games as alternate uniforms during the season.

Then & Now
MICHAEL FINLEY 1996–2005 / DEVIN HARRIS 2004–08; 2013–preser

TROPHY CASE

Championships:
2011

Franchise Leaders:

Games:
Dirk Nowitzki, 1,394

Points:
Dirk Nowitzki, 30,260

3-Pointers:
Dirk Nowitzki, 1,780

Assists:
Derek Harper 5,111

Mavs owner, 2000–present:
Mark Cuban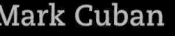

SUPERFACT

Dirk Nowitzki is as talented with a guitar as he is with his fadeaway jump shot. Not content to play just guitar, the superstar forward also began learning to play the saxophone in 2001. However, Spurs point guard Terry Porter caught him in the jaw with an elbow during a playoff game and knocked out his front tooth. The saxophone had to wait until Nowitzki could replace the tooth.

Denver NUGGETS

The Denver Nuggets started out as an ABA franchise called the Denver Larks in 1967. The team changed their name to the Denver Rockets before the first season. In 1974, the team changed names once again, this time settling on the Denver Nuggets. The Nuggets joined the NBA in 1976. The Nuggets have had 33 combined ABA/NBA playoff appearances, but they've never won a title.

WON/LOSS RECORD:
2,016–2,042 (.497 W–L%)

HOME COURT:
Pepsi Center

SUPERFACT

The Nuggets wore away jerseys that featured a "rainbow skyline" from 1981-1993. The jerseys featured the Denver skyline in multi-colored blocks against a white mountain background. Because they looked like the popular video game, fans called the uniforms the "Tetris" look.

Then & Now
KIKI VANDEWEGHE 1980–84 / DANILO GALLINARI 2011–present

TROPHY CASE

Championships:
None

Franchise Leaders:
Games:
Alex English, 837

Points:
Alex English, 21,645

Rebounds:
Dan Issel, 6,630

Blocks:
Dikembe Mutombo, 1,486

Points, rookie season:
Carmelo Anthony, 1,725

SUPERFACT

Point guard **Emmanuel Mudiay** took a wild path to the NBA. He was born in Africa's war-torn Democratic Republic of the Congo. Along with his mother and older brother, he moved to the United States as a five-year-old. After starring in high school hoops, he left to play one season with the Guangdong Southern Tigers in China before entering the NBA draft. He was chosen by the Nuggets with the seventh overall pick in 2015.

Detroit
PISTONS

The Pistons got their start in 1941 as the Fort Wayne Zollner Pistons in the National Basketball League. The team bounced around to several leagues. They joined the NBA in 1949 and officially moved to Detroit in 1957. Though the team had some early success, it wasn't until the "Bad Boys" team of the late 1980s that the Pistons brought home the NBA Championship trophy.

WON/LOSS RECORD:
2,653–2,797 (.487 W–L%)

HOME COURT:
The Palace of Auburn Hills

SUPERFACT

Shooting guard Joe Dumars donned jersey number 4 as one of the best Pistons players. After a great 14-year career and two NBA Championships, Detroit retired Dumars' number 4 jersey making him the only player in club history to wear that number.

Then & Now

DAVE BING 1966–75 / KENTAVIOUS CALDWELL-POPE 2013–present

TROPHY CASE

Championships:
1989, 1990, 2004

Franchise Leaders:
Games:
• **Joe Dumars, 1,018**

Points:
Isiah Thomas, 18,822

Rebounds:
Bill Laimbeer, 9,430

Blocks:
Ben Wallace, 1,486

Free throw percentage:
Chauncey Billups, .892

SUPERFACT

Center **Andre Drummond** wasn't a natural athlete as a child. In elementary school he saw little playing time and wasn't very coordinated. But then he grew, and he grew quickly. People took notice when he first dunked a basketball at age 12. That was the beginning of the big man's development into an NBA star.

Golden State
WARRIORS

The Warriors began in Philadelphia in 1946 as part of the Basketball Association of America (BAA), winning the league's championship. The franchise moved to San Francisco in 1962 and was renamed the Golden State Warriors in 1971. Recently, the Warriors rose to championship contender status with their 2014–15 title win.

WON/LOSS RECORD:
2,657–2,899 (.478 W–L%)

HOME COURT:
Oracle Arena

SUPERFACT

The top-selling jersey in 2015–16 was Stephen Curry's Golden State Warriors number 30 jersey. Curry's brother, Seth, and father, Dell, have also worn number 30 for various NBA teams.

Then & Now

RICK BARRY 1965–67; 1972–78 / KLAY THOMPSON 2011–present

TROPHY CASE

Championships:
1946 (BAA), 1956, 1975, 2015

Franchise Leaders:

Games:
Chris Mullin, 807

Points:
Wilt Chamberlain, 17,783

Rebounds:
Nate Thurmond, 12,771

Free throws:
Paul Arizin, 5,010

3-Pointers in a game:
Stephen Curry, 13 (2016)

SUPERFACT

Today, **Stephen Curry** is one of the best players in the NBA with many endorsement deals. His first appearance on an advertisement, however, came as a young child. Steph and his NBA-star father, Dell Curry, starred in an ad for Burger King together. In the ad, young Stephen asks his father if he can grow up to be a basketball player like him. Today, both Steph and his brother Seth are NBA players.

Houston ROCKETS

The Rockets got their start as the San Diego Rockets in 1967. After four seasons the team moved to Houston, where they have played ever since. The Houston Rockets have made the playoffs 31 out of 50 seasons and have won the NBA Championship twice behind Hall of Fame big man Hakeem Olajuwon.

WON/LOSS RECORD:
2,107–1,945 (.520 W–L%)

HOME COURT:
Toyota Center

SUPERFACT

The Rockets introduced special jerseys for the 2014–15 season, celebrating the Chinese New Year. The jerseys, which featured Chinese writing on the front, were a nod to the popularity of Chinese-born former Rocket, Yao Ming. Because of Ming, the Rockets became very popular in China.

Then & Now
HAKEEM OLAJUWON 1984–2001 / TREVOR ARIZA 2009–10; 2014–presen

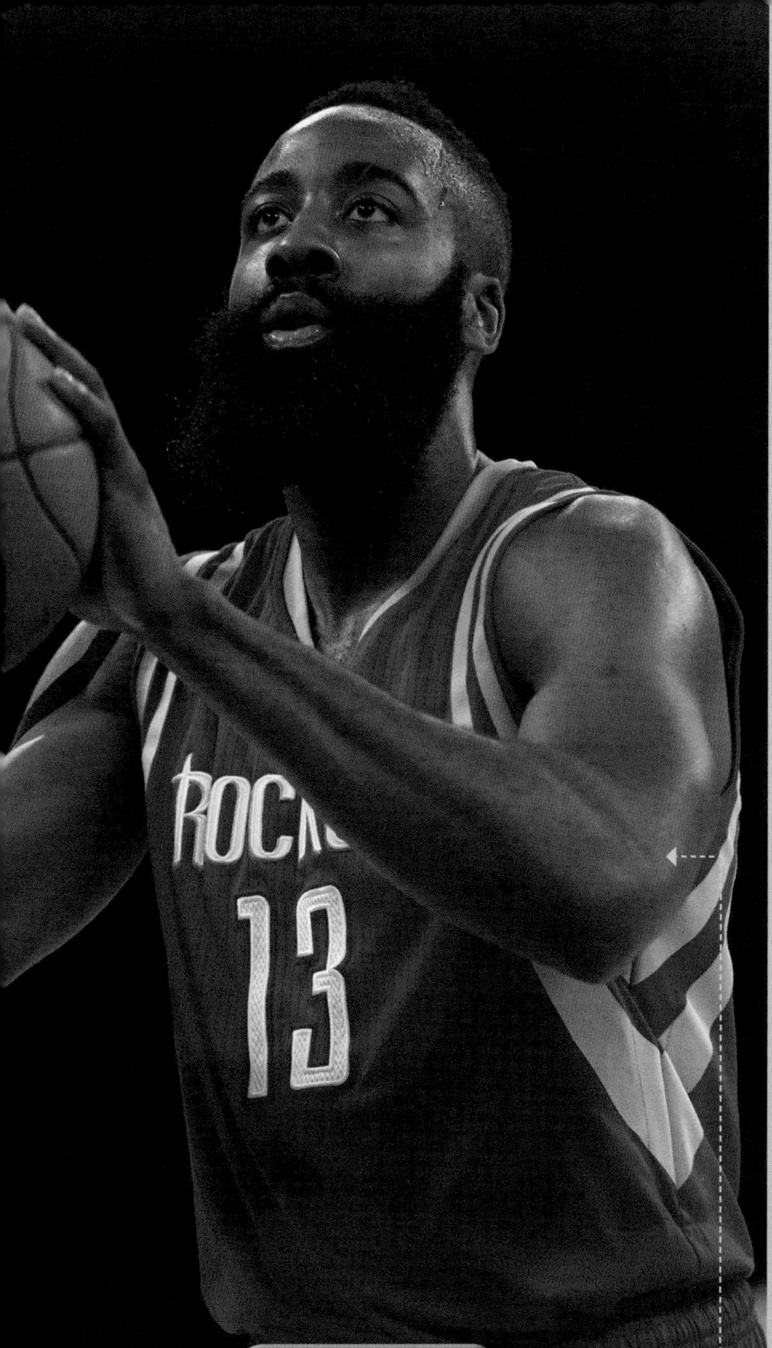

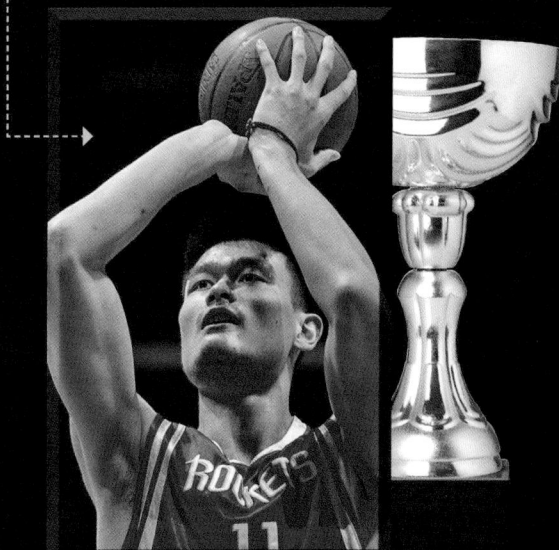

SUPERFACT

All-Star forward **James Harden** is well known for his impressive beard. Did he start growing it to be different or to create his trademark intimidating look? Nope. He began growing the beard in 2009 because he just didn't feel like shaving. As the beard grew, so did Harden's game. Today Harden is a superstar with a super beard.

TROPHY CASE

Championships:
1994, 1995

Franchise Leaders:

Games:
Hakeem Olajuwon, 1,177

Points:
Hakeem Olajuwon, 26,511

Rebounds:
Hakeem Olajuwon, 13,382

Assists:
Calvin Murphy, 4,402

Most field goals without a miss, single game:
Yao Ming, 12 (2009)

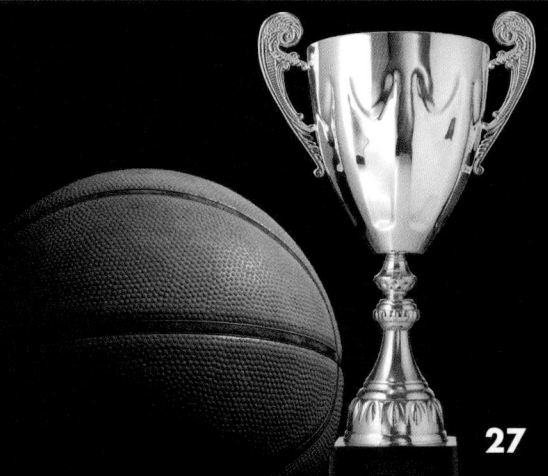

Indiana PACERS

The Indiana Pacers first took the court in 1967 as a part of the ABA. They were adopted into the NBA in 1976. While the Pacers won three Championships as a part of the ABA, they have not yet taken home the trophy in the NBA, despite making the playoffs 16 times during the 1990s and 2000s.

WON/LOSS RECORD:
2,075–1,982 (.511 W–L%)

HOME COURT:
Bankers Life Fieldhouse

SUPERFACT

During the 2015–16 season, the Pacers sometimes wore alternate uniforms. The new maroon and gold uniforms had the word "Hickory" across the front in honor of the fictional high school basketball team from the popular 1986 movie, Hoosiers.

Then & Now

RIK SMITS 1988–2000 / C.J. MILES 2014–present

TROPHY CASE

Championships:
1970, 1972, 1973 (all ABA)

Franchise Leaders:

Games:
• Reggie Miller, 1,389

Points:
Reggie Miller, 25,279

Rebounds:
Mel Daniels, 7,643

Blocks:
Jermaine O'Neal, 1,245

3-Point Field Goals:
Reggie Miller, 2,560

SUPERFACT

All-Star forward **Paul George** grew up playing basketball against his older sister, Teiosha, who played basketball at Pepperdine University. Paul claims that he couldn't beat her in a game of one-on-one until he was 17 years old. He even admits that she used to beat him so badly that he'd run into the house crying.

Los Angeles
CLIPPERS

In 1970, the NBA added three new expansion teams. One of these teams, the Buffalo Braves, moved to San Diego in 1978 and became the San Diego Clippers. In 1984 the team moved again, this time to Los Angeles. The Clippers have only made the playoffs 13 times, but they've made it each year since the 2011–12 season.

WON/LOSS RECORD:
1,520–2,286 (.399 W–L%)

HOME COURT:
Staples Center

SUPERFACT

In 2016 the Clippers introduced a new mascot, Chuck the California Condor, an endangered species of bird that lives in California. What does Chuck wear for shoes? Converse All-Stars, commonly known as "Chucks."

Then & Now
TERRY CUMMINGS 1982–84 / CHRIS PAUL 2011–present

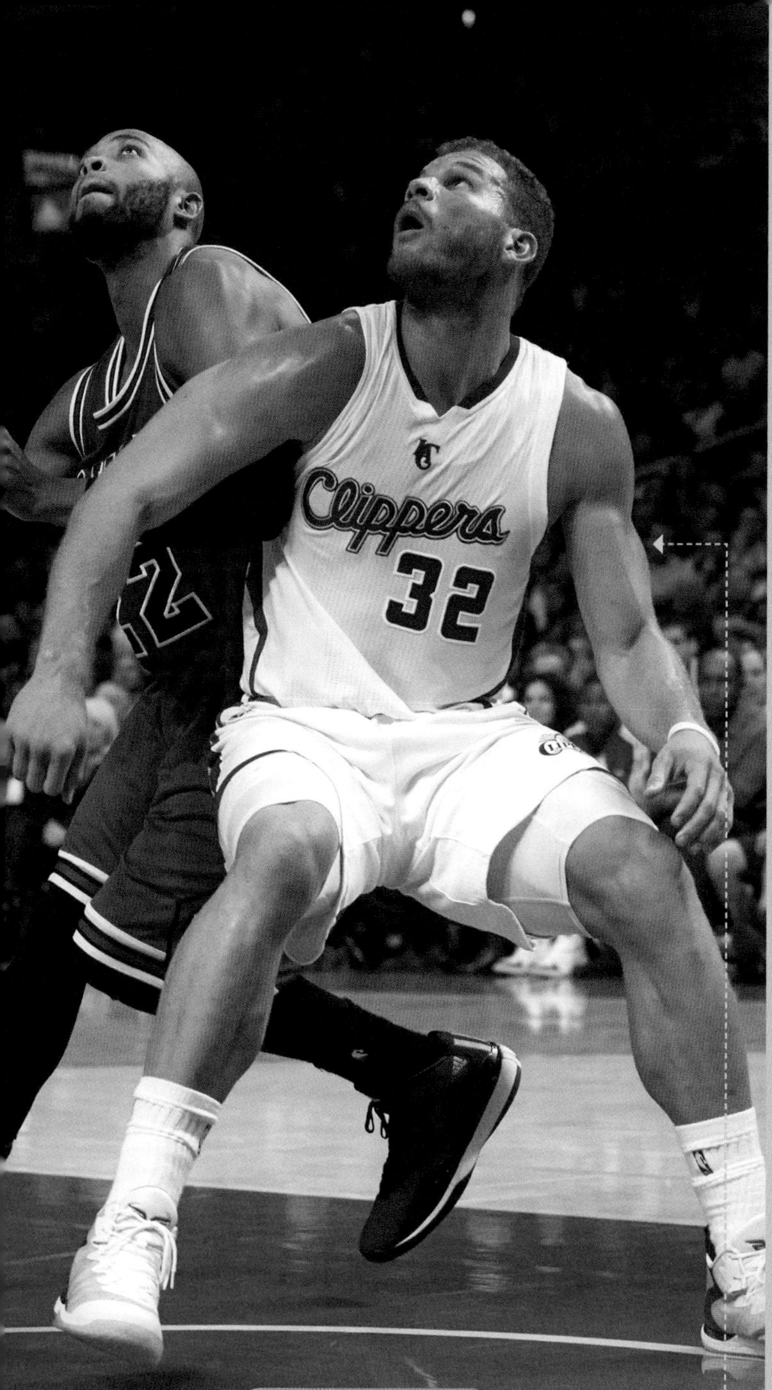

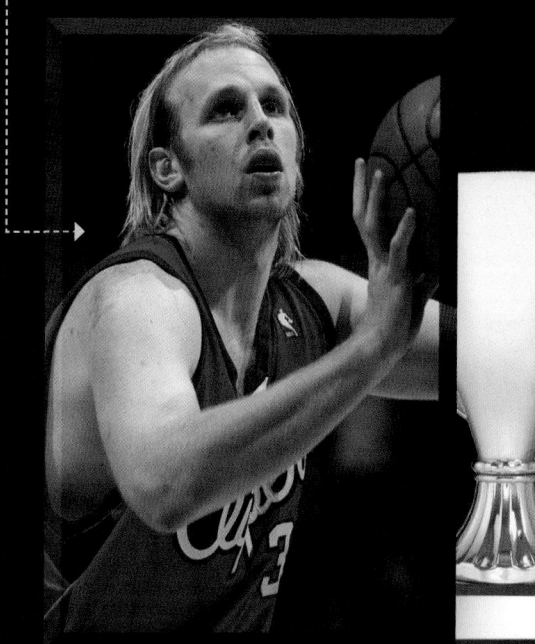

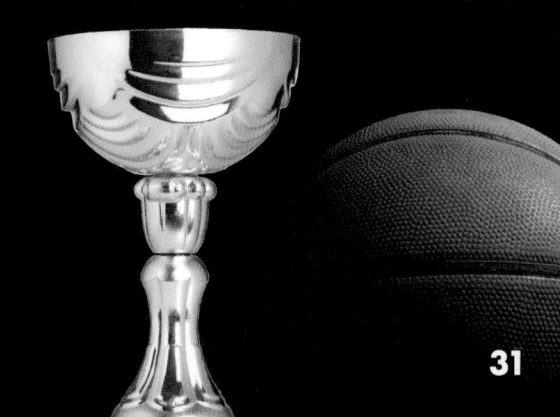

SUPERFACT

Power forward **Blake Griffin** is known for his powerful slam dunks. In the 2011 NBA Slam Dunk Contest, Griffin jumped over the hood of a KIA Optima car. It was a Slam Dunk Contest first. The high-flying dunk helped Griffin take home the trophy.

TROPHY CASE

Championships:
None

Franchise Leaders:

Games:
Randy Smith, 715

Ponts:
Randy Smith, 12,735

Assists:
Chris Paul, 4,023

3-Pointers:
Eric Piatkowski, 738

Best nickname:
Chris Kaman, "The Caveman"

Los Angeles
LAKERS

One of the oldest teams in the NBA, the Los Angeles Lakers played their first season as the Minneapolis Lakers in 1948–49. They were successful right away, winning the BAA championship their first year and the NBA title the next. The Lakers moved to L.A. in 1960 and have continued their winning tradition with a total of 16 championships.

WON/LOSS RECORD:
3,261–2,190 (.598 W–L%)

HOME COURT:
Staples Center

SUPERFACT

Current Lakers owner and former player, Jerry West, left an enduring image on the NBA. He is nicknamed "The Logo." The silhouette that is featured on the NBA logo belongs to Jerry.

Then & Now

MAGIC JOHNSON 1979–91; 1995–96 / BRANDON INGRAM 2016–present

TROPHY CASE

Championships:
1949 (BAA), 1950, 1952, 1953, 1954, 1972, 1980, 1982, 1985, 1987, 1988, 2000, 2001, 2002, 2009, 2010

Franchise Leaders:

Games:
Kobe Bryant, 1,346

Points:
Kobe Bryant, 33,643

Rebounds:
Elgin Baylor, 11,463

Assists:
Magic Johnson, 10,141

Blocks:
Kareem Abdul-Jabbar, 2,694

SUPERFACT

In his rookie season with the Lakers, **D'Angelo Russell** started 48 games, many as the backcourt mate of legendary Lakers shooting guard Kobe Bryant. Bryant, who played his final season in Russell's first, scored 60 points in his final NBA game at the age of 37. Russell had 9 points and 5 assists in the same game, a 101-96 win over the Utah Jazz.

Memphis GRIZZLIES

The Grizzlies were established in 1995 as the Vancouver Grizzlies when the NBA branched into Canada. The team moved to Memphis in 2001. The team was unsuccessful in Canada, but has made the playoffs each season since 2011 in Memphis. Led by point guard Mike Conley and center Marc Gasol, the Grizzlies built a reputation as a tough, defensive-minded team.

WON/LOSS RECORD:
737–1,019 (.420 W–L%)

HOME COURT:
FedExForum

SUPERFACT

The Grizzlies' original owners wanted to name the team the "Mounties" after the Royal Canadian Mounted Police, but both fans and the RCMP objected. The name Grizzlies was chosen as the winner from a contest in a Vancouver newspaper.

Then & Now
JASON WILLIAMS 2001–05; 2011 / MIKE CONLEY 2007–present

TROPHY CASE

Championships:
None

Franchise Leaders:

Games:
Mike Conley, 706

Points:
Mike Conley, 10,050

Rebounds:
Zach Randolph, 5,612

Blocks:
Marc Gasol, 971

Coach, first winning season:
Hubie Brown, 2003–04

SUPERFACT

Big man **Marc Gasol** started his career with the Los Angeles Lakers. He became a member of the Grizzlies in 2008, when the Lakers traded him for Pau Gasol, Marc's older brother. The two brothers faced each other for the tip-off of the 2015 All-Star Game, becoming the first brothers to do so in the NBA.

Miami
HEAT

The Miami Heat was established as an expansion franchise in the NBA in 1988. After a difficult beginning, the team acquired head coach Pat Riley and began to turn things around. Though they're one of the younger teams in the NBA with only 29 seasons played, they've made the playoffs 19 times and won the NBA Championship three times.

WON/LOSS RECORD:
1,211–1,119 (.520 W–L%)

HOME COURT:
American Airlines Arena

SUPERFACT

The Miami Heat's Mascot is a bright orange character named Burnie. His bio lists his favorite TV show as "The Three Stooges" and food as "peanut butter and Spam sandwiches."

Then & Now

ALONZO MOURNING 1995–2002; 2005–08 / GORAN DRAGIC 2015–present

Championships:
2006, 2012, 2013

Franchise Leaders:

Games:
Dwyane Wade, 855

Points:
Dwyane Wade, 20,221

Rebounds:
Udonis Haslem, 5,701

3-Point Field Goals:
Tim Hardaway, 806

First championship team:
2005–06 Miami Heat

SUPERFACT

Udonis Haslem went undrafted out of college in 2002. He worked tirelessly with NBA scout David Thorpe to develop his rebounding skills. Thorpe had a basketball that was overly inflated to make it extra bouncy. He would throw the ball at the backboard and challenge Udonis to grab it before it hit the ground. The drills worked and Udonis, a Florida native, is the Heat's all-time rebounding leader.

Milwaukee
BUCKS

The Milwaukee Bucks entered the NBA in 1968 as an expansion franchise. It didn't take them long to make their mark. They won the NBA Championship just two seasons later in 1970–71. That fast run to the NBA title was the Bucks' only time bringing home the trophy.

WON/LOSS RECORD:
2,025–1,945 (.510 W–L%)

HOME COURT:
BMO Harris Bradley Center

SUPERFACT

When Milwaukee was awarded an NBA franchise in 1968, the new owners held a contest to name the team. The "Bucks" actually came in second place. The name that received the most votes was the "Robins."

Then & Now
OSCAR ROBERTSON 1970–74 / JABARI PARKER 2014–present

TROPHY CASE

Championships:
1971

Franchise Leaders:

Games: **Junior Bridgeman, 711**

Points:
Kareem Abdul-Jabbar, 14,211

Rebounds:
Kareem Abdul-Jabbar, 7,161

3-Point Field Goals:
Ray Allen, 1,051

Free throws:
Sidney Moncrief, 3,505

SUPERFACT

Although **Giannis Antetokounmpo** was born in Greece, he had no official papers until he was 18 years old. His parents were immigrants from Nigeria, and Giannis and his brothers did not automatically qualify for Greek citizenship. The "Greek Freak" officially gained his citizenship in 2013.

Minnesota
TIMBERWOLVES

Minnesota had to wait almost 29 years after the Lakers moved to Los Angeles to have an NBA franchise once again. The Timberwolves took the court as an expansion franchise in 1989. The team has only made eight playoff appearances, with all of them coming between 1997–2004 under head coach Flip Saunders.

WON/LOSS RECORD:
878–1,370 (.391 W–L%)

HOME COURT:
Target Center

SUPERFACT

Kevin Garnett chose jersey number 21 as a tribute to his friend Malik Sealy, who wore the number in college. Sealy was killed in a car accident leaving Garnett's 24th birthday party. Fittingly, Garnett retired after 21 years in the league.

Then & Now

KEVIN GARNETT 1995–2007; 2015–16 / KARL-ANTHONY TOWNS 2015–presen

TROPHY CASE

Championships:
None

Franchise Leaders:

Games:
Kevin Garnett, 970

Points:
Kevin Garnett, 19,201

Rebounds:
Kevin Garnett, 10,718

Steals:
Kevin Garnett, 1,315

Blocks:
Kevin Garnett, 1,590

Assists, single game:
Ricky Rubio, 19 (2017)

SUPERFACT

At the NBA combine, each player going into the draft is measured for a variety of skills. **Andrew Wiggins** astonished viewers with a 44-inch vertical leap. His leaping ability became so famous that the Internet has a series of memes showing him leaping up to touch things like the Statue of Liberty's torch and the tip of the Eiffel Tower.

New Orleans
PELICANS

The New Orleans Pelicans started out in 1987 as the Charlotte Hornets. After failed attempts to lure other NBA franchises to New Orleans, the NBA finally approved the sale of the Hornets to the city in 2001. The team played as the New Orleans Hornets until changing their name to the Pelicans before the 2013–2014 season.

WON/LOSS RECORD:
562–652 (.463 W–L%)

HOME COURT:
Smoothie King Center

SUPERFACT

When New Orleans changed their team name to the Pelicans, it came with a new mascot. However, the original Pierre the Pelican frightened children. In 2014 the club gave the mascot a new, fan-friendly makeover.

Then & Now

CHRIS PAUL 2005–11 / DEMARCUS COUSINS 2017–present

TROPHY CASE

Championships:
None

Franchise Leaders:

Games:
David West, 530

Points:
David West, 8,690

Rebounds:
David West, 3,853

Assists:
Chris Paul, 4,228

Blocks:
Anthony Davis, 793

SUPERFACT

Pelicans superstar **Anthony Davis** is known for his elite scoring, devastating blocked shots, and his "unibrow." Before entering the NBA, Davis trademarked his unibrow along with the phrases "Raise the Brow" and "Fear the Brow." Davis's own mother has been seen wearing a "Fear the Brow" T-shirt at games.

New York KNICKS

The New York Knickerbockers were one of the original 11 teams in the Basketball Association of America (BAA) in 1946 and joined the NBA before the 1949–50 season. As one of the oldest teams in NBA history, the Knicks have a storied history. The Knicks have been to the playoffs 42 times and captured a pair of NBA titles.

WON/LOSS RECORD:
2,732–2,825 (.492 W–L%)

HOME COURT:
Madison Square Garden

SUPERFACT

The team name "Knickerbockers" was literally drawn out of a hat. Team executives each wrote down a team name and then put it in a hat. After they drew the name, they realized that almost all the names suggested were the same. The Knickerbocker was a very popular symbol in New York at the time.

Then & Now

WILLIS REED 1964–74 / CARMELO ANTHONY 2011–17

TROPHY CASE

Championships:
1970, 1973

Franchise Leaders:

Games:
Patrick Ewing, 1,039

Points:
Patrick Ewing, 23,665

Rebounds:
Patrick Ewing, 10,759

Assists:
Walt Frazier, 4,791

Steals:
Patrick Ewing, 1,061

Blocks:
Patrick Ewing, 2,758

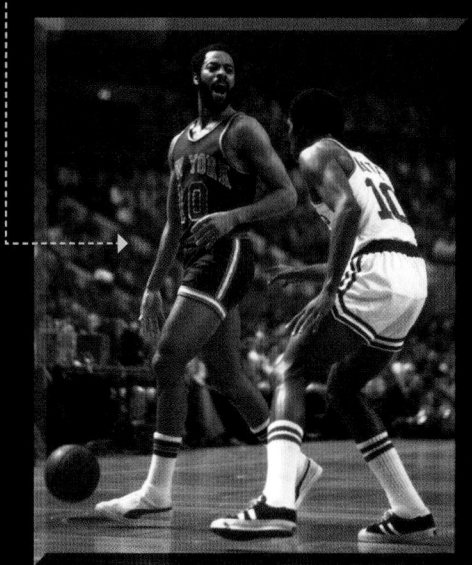

SUPERFACT

When New York took **Kristaps Porzingis** with the fourth pick of the 2015 NBA Draft, Knicks fans booed loudly. Porzingis, though, was thrilled to be a Knick and promised to change fans' minds. On the court he proved to be a deadly shooter and a determined force underneath the basket. He finished second in NBA Rookie of the Year voting and has quickly become one of the most popular players on the Knicks roster.

Oklahoma City THUNDER

The Thunder used to make noise in Seattle as the Supersonics. The team originated in 1967 and played 41 seasons in the Great Northwest before moving to Oklahoma City and changing its name to the Thunder in 2008. OKC, as it is affectionately known, has as rabid a fanbase as did Sonics teams in Seattle.

WON/LOSS RECORD:
2,186–1,866 (.539 W–L%)

HOME COURT:
Chesapeake Energy Arena

SUPERFACT

Oklahoma City chose the Thunder as its nickname over five other names. The others were Wind, Barons, Energy, Bison, and Marshalls. Thunder was considered a great choice because of the many storms that occur in Oklahoma's "Tornado Alley." Also, Oklahoma City's 45th Infantry Division is referred to as the Thunderbirds.

Then & Now

VLADIMIR RADMANOVIC 2001-06 / **STEVEN ADAMS** 2013-present

TROPHY CASE

Championships:
1979

Franchise Leaders:

Games:
Gary Payton, 999

Points:
Gary Payton, 18, 207

Rebounds:
Jack Sikma, 7,729

3-Point Field Goals:
Kevin Durant, 1,143

Assists:
Gary Payton, 7,384

Blocks:
Serge Ibaka, 1,300

SUPERFACT

Like many athletes, **Russell Westbrook** has his preferred pregame meal. Before each tip-off, Westbrook eats a peanut butter and jelly sandwich. He's very particular about it. It must be made with Skippy peanut butter, strawberry jelly, on toasted wheat bread, and cut in half diagonally. It seems to be working for the all-star.

Orlando
MAGIC

The Magic first appeared in the NBA in 1989 as an expansion franchise. Orlando made it to the NBA Finals in just its sixth season on the court, but came up short against the Houston Rockets. Big name stars such as Shaquille O'Neal, Penny Hardaway, and Dwight Howard have started their careers with the Orlando Magic.

WON/LOSS RECORD:
1,091–1,157 (.484 W–L%)

HOME COURT:
Amway Center

SUPERFACT

The Orlando Magic has only retired one jersey number and it wasn't to honor a player. The team retired the number 6 in honor of their fans, whom they call their "sixth man."

Then & Now

PENNY HARDAWAY 1993–99 / ELFRID PAYTON 2014–present

TROPHY CASE

Championships:
None

Franchise Leaders:

Games:
Nick Anderson, 692

Points:
Dwight Howard, 11,435

Rebounds:
Dwight Howard, 8,072

3-Pointers:
Dennis Scott, 981

Assists:
Jameer Nelson, 3,501

SUPERFACT

No one wants to pick a fight with forward **Evan Fournier**. Growing up in France, both his parents were judo instructors. Evan studied judo, as well as basketball, as a child until he needed to choose one. He wisely chose basketball, but still has a few judo skills.

Philadelphia
76ERS

One of the oldest teams in the NBA, the Philadelphia 76ers were founded in 1946 as the Syracuse Nationals. The team was purchased and moved to Philadelphia in 1963. The team's long history is rich with superstars like Wilt Chamberlain, Julius Erving, and Allen Iverson. The 76ers have won three NBA championships.

WON/LOSS RECORD:
2,754–2,632 (.511 W–L%)

HOME COURT:
Wells Fargo Center

SUPERFACT

In 2016 the 76ers released photos of a new jersey featuring a small advertisement from Stubhub sewn on. It is the first major sports jersey to sell ad space. Since then, other teams have joined the trend, including the Kings, Celtics, and others.

Then & Now
JULIUS ERVING 1976–87 / DARIO SARIC 2016–present

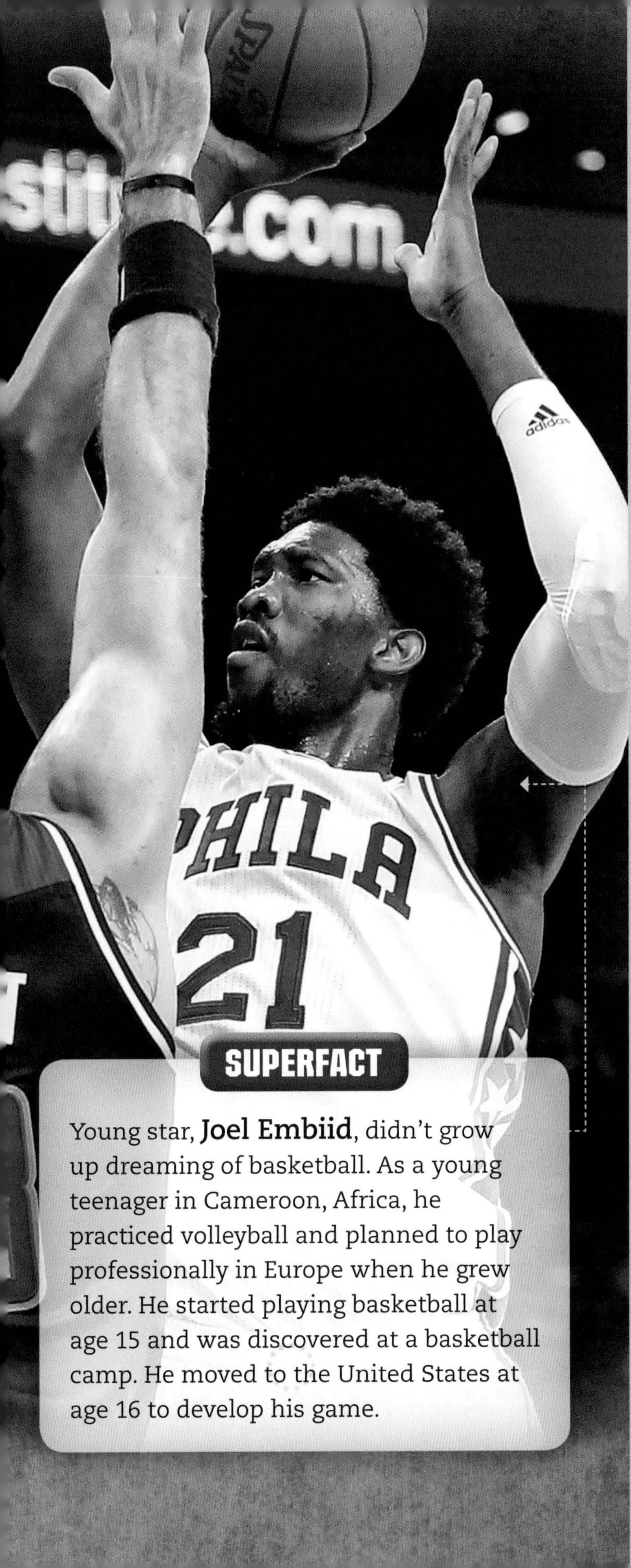

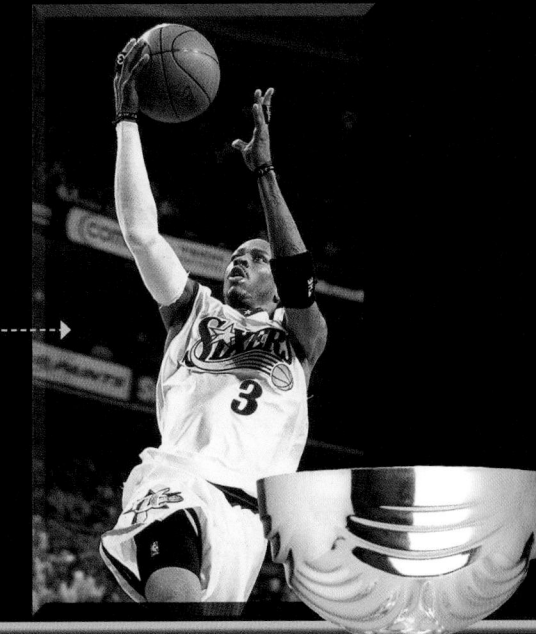

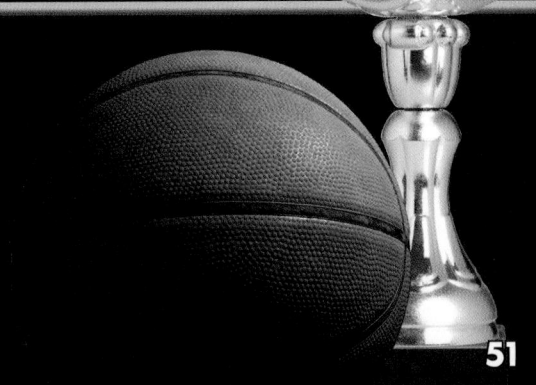

SUPERFACT

Young star, **Joel Embiid**, didn't grow up dreaming of basketball. As a young teenager in Cameroon, Africa, he practiced volleyball and planned to play professionally in Europe when he grew older. He started playing basketball at age 15 and was discovered at a basketball camp. He moved to the United States at age 16 to develop his game.

TROPHY CASE

Championships:
1955, 1967, 1983

Franchise Leaders:

Games:
Hal Greer, 1,122

Points:
Hal Greer, 21,586

Rebounds:
Dolph Schayes, 11,256

Assists:
Maurice Cheeks, 6,212

Blocks:
Julius Erving, 1,293

3-Point Field Goals:
Allen Iverson, 885

Phoenix SUNS

The Phoenix Suns were established in 1968 as an expansion team in the NBA. The Suns have made it to the NBA Finals twice, but came up short each time. Stars such as Charles Barkley, Paul Westphal, Kevin Johnson, and Steve Nash have all suited up for the Suns.

WON/LOSS RECORD:
2,146–1,824 (.541 W–L%)

HOME COURT:
Talking Stick Resort Arena

SUPERFACT

The Phoenix Suns Gorilla is one of the most recognized mascots in the NBA, but he started out as an accident. Henry Rojas was at a game in 1980, wearing a gorilla costume as part of a singing telegram delivery. He danced on the court and the crowd loved him.

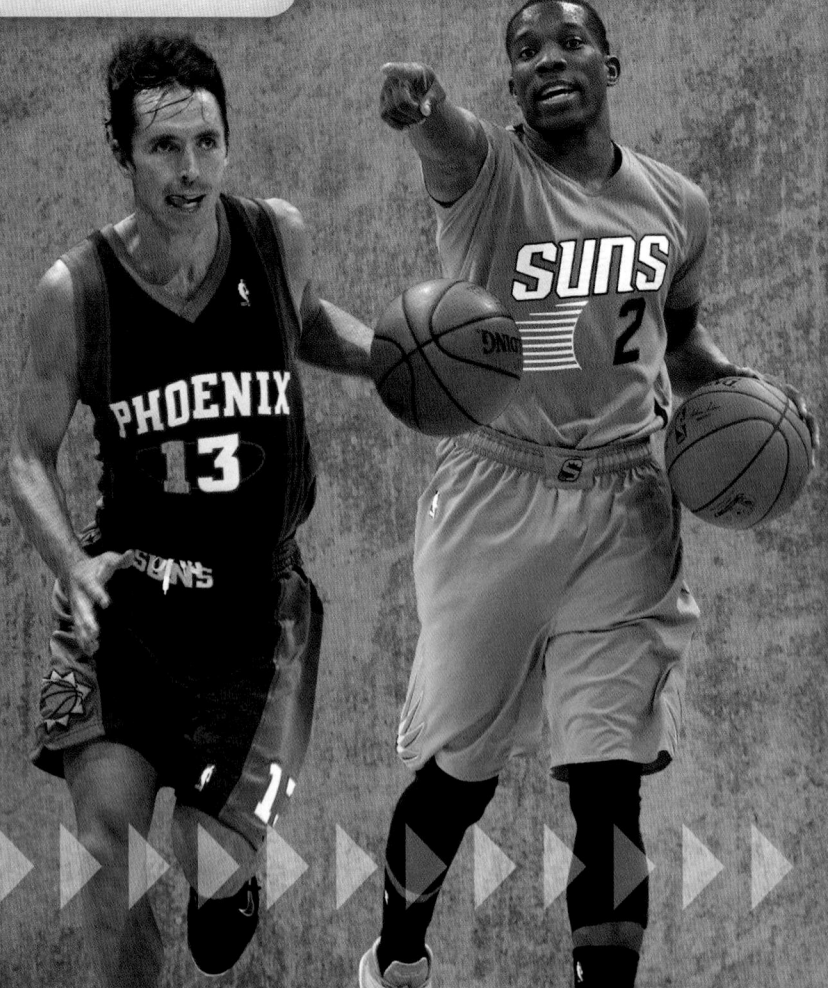

Then & Now
STEVE NASH 1996–98; 2004–12 / ERIC BLEDSOE 2013–present

Championships:
None

Franchise Leaders:

Games:
Alvan Adams, 988

Points:
Walter Davis, 15,666

Rebounds:
Alvan Adams, 6,937

Assists:
Steve Nash, 6,997

Free throws, single season:
Amar'e Stoudemire, 583 (2004–05)

SUPERFACT

Devin Booker was born to be an NBA star. His father, Melvin Booker, played briefly in the NBA and then professionally in Europe. When he saw the talent that his son had, he quit his career early to help guide Devin. The move paid off. Devin proved his worth, setting the single-game Suns' scoring record with 70 points versus the Celtics on March 24, 2017.

Portland
TRAIL BLAZERS

The Portland Trail Blazers joined the NBA in 1970. After six consecutive losing seasons, the Blazers turned it around by winning the NBA Finals in 1976–77, their first year reaching the playoffs. The club has been a consistently strong team ever since, but has not won the Finals a second time.

WON/LOSS RECORD:
2,032–1,774 (.534 W–L%)

HOME COURT:
Moda Center

SUPERFACT

When the Trail Blazers won a big game against the Lakers in 1966 with a last-second shot, radio play-by-play man Bill Schonely shouted, "Rip City, all right!" The nickname "Rip City" has stuck with the Trail Blazers ever since.

Then & Now
BILL WALTON 1974–78 / C.J. MCCOLLUM 2013–present

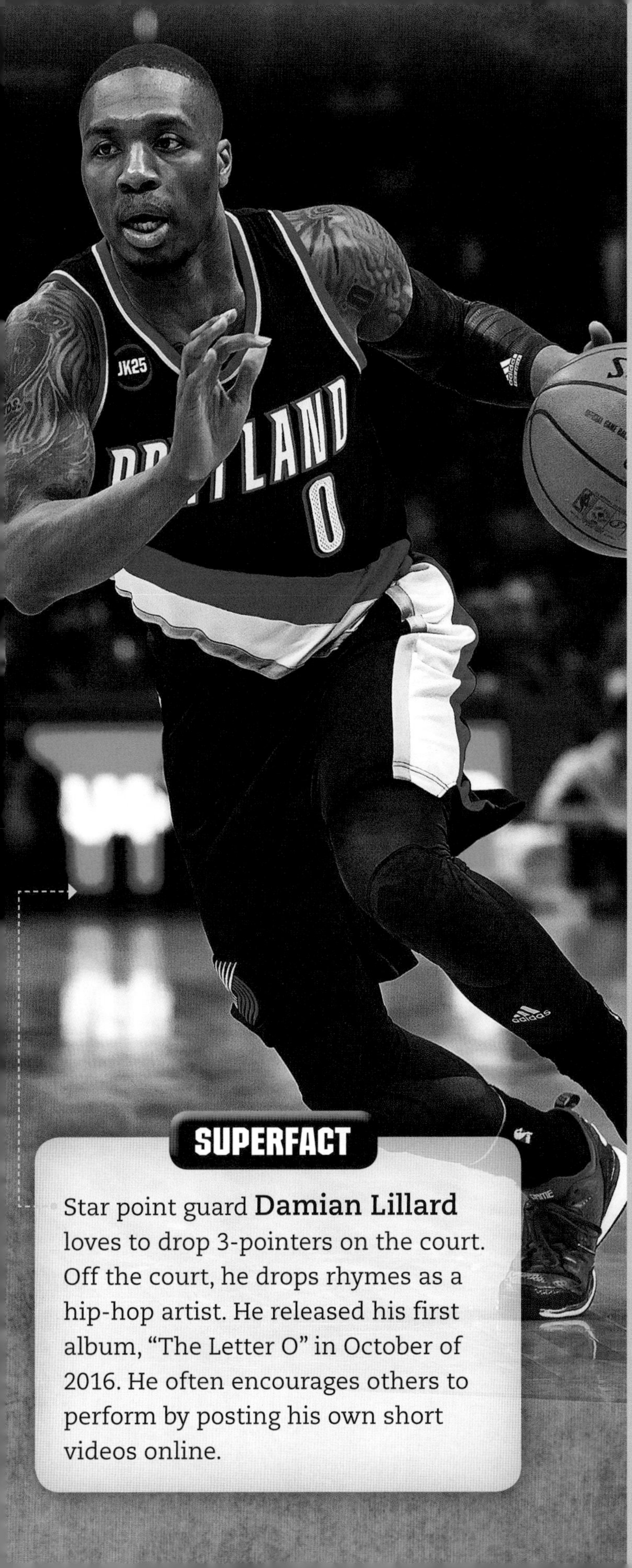

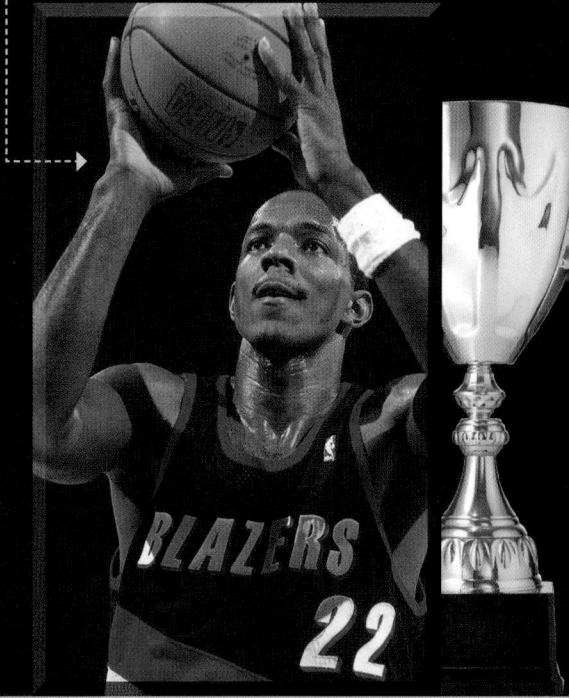

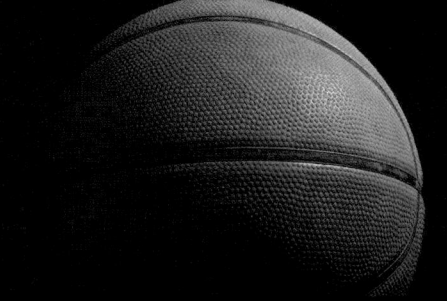

SUPERFACT

Star point guard **Damian Lillard** loves to drop 3-pointers on the court. Off the court, he drops rhymes as a hip-hop artist. He released his first album, "The Letter O" in October of 2016. He often encourages others to perform by posting his own short videos online.

TROPHY CASE

Championships:

1977

Franchise Leaders:

Games:
Clyde Drexler, 867

Points:
Clyde Drexler, 18,040

Rebounds:
LaMarcus Aldridge, 5,434

3-Pointers:
Damian Lillard, 1,042

Assists:
Terry Porter, 5,319

Blocks:
Mychal Thompson, 768

Sacramento KINGS

The Sacramento Kings are a well-traveled franchise. Originally created as the Rochester Royals in 1948, the club has also existed as the Cincinnati Royals, the Kansas City-Omaha Kings, and the Kansas City Kings. The team found its current home in Sacramento, California, in 1985.

WON/LOSS RECORD:
2,496–2,955 (.458 W–L%)

HOME COURT:
Golden 1 Center

SUPERFACT

Slamson the Lion has been the Kings' mascot for years. He has his own Facebook page and Twitter account.

Then & Now

CHRIS WEBBER 1998–2005 / WILLIE CAULEY-STEIN 2015–present

Championships:
1951

Franchise Leaders:

Games:
Sam Lacey, 888

Points:
Oscar Robertson, 22,009

Rebounds:
Sam Lacey, 9,353

3-Point Field Goals:
Peja Stojakovic, 1,070

Assists:
Oscar Robertson, 7,731

Former player/current GM:
• **Vlade Divac**

SUPERFACT

Kings shooting guard **Buddy Hield** didn't grow up wearing the latest superstar-endorsed basketball shoes. He was born to a poor family in a rough part of the Bahamas. Regardless, Hield fell in love with basketball and worked relentlessly to improve his game. Very competitive on the court, Hield is the king of laughter and smiles off of it. He calls himself "Buddy Buckets" when playing and "Buddy Fresh" off the court for different personality styles.

San Antonio SPURS

The San Antonio Spurs started out as the Dallas Chaparrals of the ABA. The team moved to San Antonio 1973 and took on the name the Spurs. They joined the NBA through the ABA/NBA merger in 1976. The Spurs have been one of the most consistent teams in the entire league, making the playoffs a remarkable 45 times in just 50 seasons.

WON/LOSS RECORD:
2,445–1,613 (.603 W–L%)

HOME COURT:
AT&T Center

SUPERFACT

David Robinson chose the jersey number 50 to be like his idol, 7 foot 4 inch tall Ralph Sampson. Robinson did the number justice by eclipsing his idol in nearly every statistical category.

Then & Now
GEORGE GERVIN 1974–85 / TONY PARKER 2001–present

TROPHY CASE

Championships:
- 1999, 2003, 2005, 2007, 2014

Franchise Leaders:

Games:
Tim Duncan, 1,392

Points:
Tim Duncan, 26,496

Rebounds:
Tim Duncan, 15,091

3-Point Field Goals:
Manu Ginobili, 1,431

Assists:
Tony Parker, 6,634

Steals:
David Robinson, 1,388

SUPERFACT

Spurs superstar **Kawhi Leonard** didn't play basketball his freshman year of high school. He tried to, but missed tryouts because he didn't have a ride. Even though he explained the situation to his coach, the coach didn't let it slide and wouldn't let Kawhi play. Instead, Kawhi went out for football that season.

Toronto
RAPTORS

The Toronto Raptors, the NBA's only team in Canada, joined the league in 1995. In just over two decades of play, the Raptors have had some of the NBA's most exciting players, including Vince Carter, Chris Bosh, and Kyle Lowry. The young franchise has not yet made it to the NBA Finals.

WON/LOSS RECORD:
785–971 (.447 W–L%)

HOME COURT:
Air Canada Centre

SUPERFACT

When Toronto was granted an expansion franchise in 1993, the NBA held a naming contest to decide the team's nickname. The Raptors won out largely due to the popularity of the movie *Jurassic Park* during that time.

Then & Now

VINCE CARTER 1998–2004 / DEMAR DEROZAN 2009–present

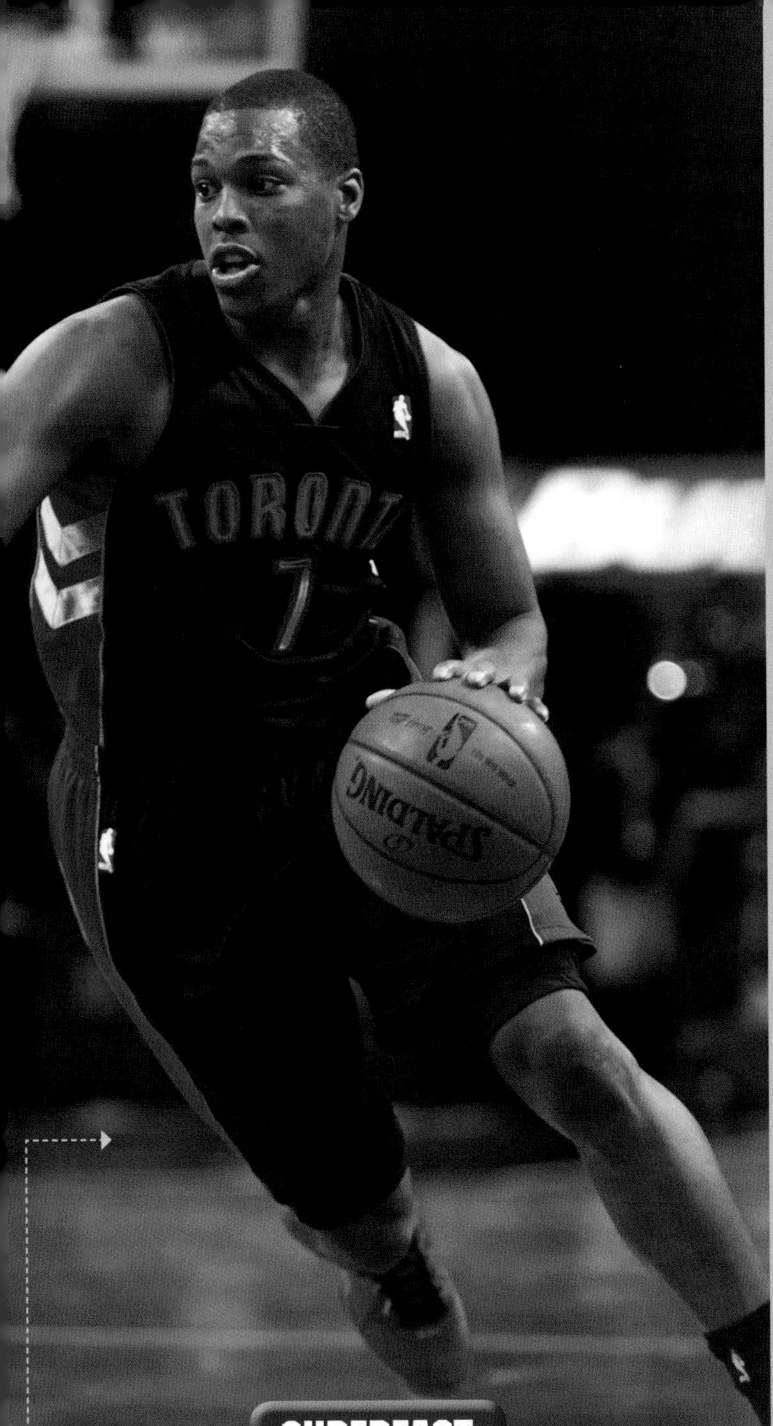

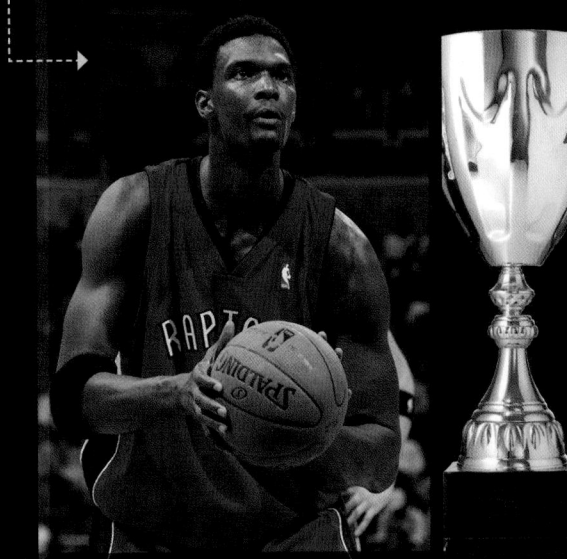

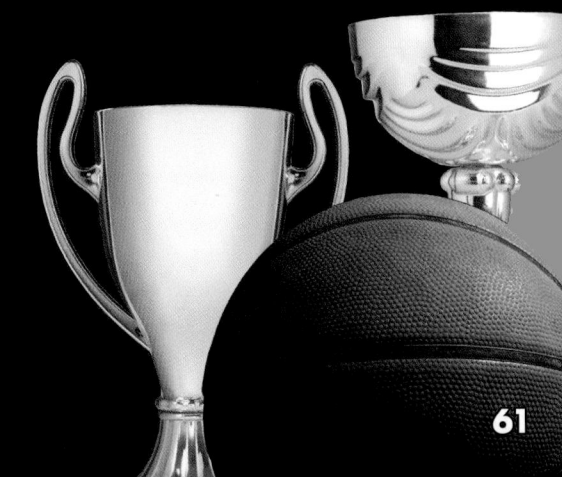

SUPERFACT

Kyle Lowry and DeMar DeRozan work well together on the court. Off the court, the pair are good friends that like to pick on each other during interviews. They even star in some television ads together, showing off the chemistry that makes them such a unique pair of teammates.

TROPHY CASE

Championships:

None

Franchise Leaders:

Games:
DeMar DeRozan, 595

Points:
DeMar DeRozan, 11,456

Rebounds:
Chris Bosh, 4,776

Assists:
Jose Calderon, 3,770

Blocks:
Chris Bosh, 600

Utah
JAZZ

The Jazz got their start in the Big Easy as the New Orleans Jazz in 1974. The franchise moved to Utah in 1979. After missing the playoffs in their first nine seasons, the Jazz have been a consistent presence in the NBA postseason.

WON/LOSS RECORD:
1,866–1,612 (.537 W–L%)

HOME COURT:
Vivint Smart Home Arena

SUPERFACT

In 2014 the Jazz retired the number 1223, representing the number of victories legendary head coach Jerry Sloan accumulated during his time with the team.

Then & Now

ANDREI KIRILENKO 2001–11 / RUDY GOBERT 2013–present

TROPHY CASE

Championships:
None

Franchise Leaders:
Games:
John Stockton, 1,504

Points:
Karl Malone, 36,374

Rebounds:
Karl Malone, 14,601

3-Point Field Goals:
John Stockton, 845

Assists:
John Stockton, 15,806

SUPERFACT

Jazz forward **Gordon Hayward** dreamed of being a basketball player when he grew up. As a kid, though, he was not deemed tall enough. He played tennis doubles with his sister and thought about focusing on tennis instead of hoops. Then he hit a growth spurt and his basketball dreams became a reality.

Washington
WIZARDS

The Washington Wizards started out as the Chicago Packers in 1961. The team bounced around from Chicago to Baltimore and finally to Washington where they became the Washington Bullets. The Bullets won the NBA Championship in 1977–78. The team changed its nickname to the Wizards in 1997.

WON/LOSS RECORD:
2,053–2,480 (.453 W–L%)

HOME COURT:
Verizon Center

SUPERFACT

In September of 2001, Wizards fans were thrilled to learn that legendary shooting guard Michael Jordan would be coming out of his second retirement to play for their team. Jordan wore jersey number 23 for the Wizards, just as he had during his career with the Chicago Bulls. When Jordan retired for good, he did so as the all-time king of NBA jersey sales.

Then & Now
MICHAEL JORDAN 2001–03 / BRADLEY BEAL 2012–present

TROPHY CASE

Championships: 1978

Franchise Leaders:

Games:
Wes Unseld, 984

Points:
Elvin Hayes, 15,551

Rebounds:
Wes Unseld, 13,769

3-Point Field Goals:
Gilbert Arenas, 868

Assists:
John Wall, 4,610

SUPERFACT

Star point guard **John Wall** is known for dishing out great assists and showing off his famous "John Wall Dance." The simple dance involves holding one fist in the air and turning it back and forth. The move became so popular that a hip-hop group called Troop 41 released a single called, "Do the John Wall."

ALL-TIME PRO BASKETBALL LEADERS

REGULAR SEASON

GAMES

1. Robert Parish – 1,611
2. Kareem Abdul-Jabbar – 1,560
3. John Stockton – 1,504
4. Karl Malone – 1,476
5. Kevin Garnett – 1,462
6. Moses Malone – 1,455
7. Kevin Willis – 1,424
8. Dirk Nowitzki – 1,394*
9. Tim Duncan – 1,392
10. Jason Kidd – 1,391

POINTS

1. Kareem Abdul-Jabbar – 38,387
2. Karl Malone – 36,928
3. Kobe Bryant – 33,643
4. Michael Jordan – 32,292
5. Wilt Chamberlain – 31,419
6. Dirk Nowitzki – 30,260*
7. Julius Erving – 30,026
8. Moses Malone – 29,580
9. LeBron James – 28,787*
10. Shaquille O'Neal – 28,596

REBOUNDS

1. Wilt Chamberlain – 23,924
2. Bill Russell – 21,620
3. Moses Malone – 17,834
4. Kareem Abdul-Jabbar – 17,440
5. Artis Gilmore – 16,330
6. Elvin Hayes – 16,279
7. Tim Duncan – 15,091
8. Karl Malone – 15,968
9. Robert Parish – 14,715
10. Kevin Garnett – 14,662

ASSISTS

1. John Stockton – 15,806
2. Jason Kidd – 12,091
3. Steve Nash – 10,335
4. Mark Jackson – 10,334
5. Magic Johnson – 10,141
6. Oscar Robertson – 9,887
7. Isiah Thomas – 9,061
8. Gary Payton – 8,966
9. Andre Miller – 8,524
10. Chris Paul – 8,251*

3-POINT FIELD GOALS

1. Ray Allen – 2,973
2. Reggie Miller – 2,560
3. Jason Terry – 2,242*
4. Paul Pierce – 2,143
5. Kyle Korver – 2,049*
5. Vince Carter – 2,049*
5. Jamal Crawford – 2,049*
8. Jason Kidd – 1,988
9. Joe Johnson – 1,938*
10. Stephen Curry – 1,917*

BLOCKS

1. Hakeem Olajuwon – 3,830
2. Dikembe Mutombo – 3,289
3. Kareem Abdul-Jabbar – 3,189
4. Artis Gilmore – 3,178
5. Mark Eaton – 3,064
6. Tim Duncan – 3,020
7. David Robinson – 2,954
8. Patrick Ewing – 2,894
9. Shaquille O'Neal – 2,732
10. Tree Rollins – 2,542

* still active

NBA FINALS LEADERS

GAMES

1. Bill Russell – 70
2. Sam Jones – 64
3. Kareem Abdul-Jabbar – 56
4. Jerry West – 55
5. Tom Heinsohn – 52

POINTS

1. Jerry West – 1,679
2. Kareem Abdul-Jabbar – 1,317
3. Michael Jordan – 1,176
4. Elgin Baylor – 1,161
5. Bill Russell – 1,151

MOST NBA FINALS MVPS

1. Michael Jordan – 6
2. Magic Johnson – 3
2. Shaquille O'Neal – 3
2. Tim Duncan – 3
2. LeBron James – 3

MOST NBA TITLES (INDIVIDUAL)

1. Bill Russell – 11
2. Sam Jones – 10
3. John Havlicek – 8
3. Tom Heinsohn – 8
3. K.C. Jones – 8
3. Tom Sanders - 8

MOST NBA TITLES (TEAM)

1. Boston Celtics – 17
2. Los Angeles Lakers – 16
3. Chicago Bulls - 6

READ MORE

Bryant, Howard. *Legends: The Best Players, Games, and Teams in Basketball.* Legends 3. New York: Philomel Books, 2017.

Editors of Sports Illustrated Kids. *Big Book of Who Basketball.* Sports Illustrated Kids Big Books. New York: Time Home Entertainment, 2015.

Forest, Christopher. *Side-by-Side Basketball Stars: Comparing Pro Basketball's Greatest Players.* Side-by-Side Sports. North Mankato, Minn.: Capstone Press, 2015.

INTERNET SITES

Use FactHound to find Internet sites related to this book.

Visit www.facthound.com

Just type in 9781515788508 and go.

Portland Trail
Blazers

Sacramento
Kings

Golden State
Warriors

Utah Jazz

Denver
Nuggets

Los Angeles
Clippers

Oklahoma City
Thunder

Phoenix
Suns

Los Angeles
Lakers

Dallas
Mavericks

San Antonio
Spurs

Minnesota Timberwolves

Milwaukee Bucks

Toronto Raptors

Detroit Pistons

Boston Celtics

Brooklyn Nets
New York Knicks

Chicago Bulls

Cleveland Cavaliers

Philadelphia 76ers

Washington Wizards

Indiana Pacers

Charlotte Hornets

Memphis Grizzlies

Atlanta Hawks

New Orleans Pelicans

Houston Rockets

Orlando Magic

Miami Heat

INDEX